BARS

Set Free by God's Invisible Hand

BARS

Set Free by God's Invisible Hand

Bettina J. D. Woodard

BARS Copyright ©2017 Bettina J. D. Woodard

All rights reserved under International Copyright Law. This book may not be copied or reprinted for commercial gain or profit.

Unless otherwise indicated, Scriptures are taken from the New International Version.

Every precaution has been taken to change the names and locations mentioned in this book. This story is based on a real-life experience and is not meant to expose or harm anyone. Parental guidance is advised; this book contains subject matter that is not suitable for young children.

ISBN 978-1-941749-73-9
Library of Congress Control Number 2017913940

Cover Design: Michael Simmons
Illustrator: Tiffany L. Woodard
Interior Design: Laura Brown
Mentor: Dr. Sharon Cannon
Editor: Sylvia Banks
S.W.A.T. Book Camp: Coach Laura Brown

4-P Publishing
Chattanooga, TN 37411
Printed in the United States of America

DEDICATION

I dedicate this book to Tiffany L. and Valeesa E. Woodard.

It is my prayer that God will continue to bless you and protect you from harm and pain. May He give you wisdom and discernment to know right from wrong and surround you with like-minded people. May the Lord bless you with total health, body, soul, and mind. May God bless your dreams, everything your hand's touch, and everywhere your feet tread, in the name of Jesus' strips and blood. I love you both, dearly.

SPECIAL DEDICATION

My oldest brother, Garland Moore, died suddenly while I was writing this book. He will be missed and loved. I thank him for serving our country in the United States Army.

ACKNOWLEDGMENTS

I thank God for the people who were pleasant, unpleasant, and downright ugly. Each experience led to a life-changing metamorphosis used to teach, strengthen, heal, and restore.

Because of God, Jesus, The Holy Spirit, and the people assigned to me, this book exists.

Did I have doubt? Yes. My faith was that of a mustard seed, which God requires. He met my needs, as I worked to complete the book, *BARS*, in spite of my adversities. I placed everything in God's hands so He could fight for me.

The Lord will fight for you; you need only to be still. (Exodus 14:14)

A Note from the Author

Dear Friend,

This book, *BARS*, is about my life. The title is symbolic because, for many years of my life, I felt as though I was a prisoner behind BARS. Every hurt, pain, disappointment, and rejection that I encountered erected invisible bars that held me back living a cyclical life, going around in circles and ending nowhere.

Maybe you too, my friend, have experienced atrocities in your life, things that were out of your control but a part of your environment. Perhaps, like me, you accepted the abnormal as normal.

I write my story as a testimony of healing and moving forward. I realize the past has gone and there's nothing I can do to change it. However, the future is ahead of me and that my friend, gives me hope to make each day count!

At the end of each chapter, you will find a place to record your reflections. You can add a date and time. I pray you will find healing in journaling.

I have renewed hope and faith in God. I pray that you too, will receive hope and healing for your situations and keep moving forward. All things are possible with God.

After Reading *BARS*, please write your review at Amazon.com, thank you.

You can connect with me at:
bettinawoodard141414@gmail.com

Table of Contents

SETTING AND CAST OF CHARACTERS 11

MY REARVIEW MIRROR 15

HURT 25

   REJECTION 35

FEAR 47

   UNCERTAINTY 57

PRIDE 71

SHAME 87

   DIVORCE 99

   FREEDOM 123

SCRIPTURES ON FORGIVENESS 135

HEALING SCRIPTURES 141

NATIONAL STATISTICS ON CHILD ABUSE 147

SETTING AND CAST OF CHARACTERS

The setting for this story is Helltown, TN. (This is a fictitious place, but it sure was real to me.) These are the people you will meet in this book:

- Harry—father
- Sue—mother
- Sally—my alter ego (This is the mask I wore.)
- Entourage of friends
- Children
- Daughters
- Brother
- Sister
- The Principal
- Derrick
- Lawless People (citizens of Helltown and people anyone could meet.)

"The soul is the master of a person because man's will is part of the soul. When the spirit controls the whole being, it is because the soul has yielded itself and has taken a lower position. If the soul rebels, the spirit will not have the power to control it. This is the meaning of "free will" in man. Man has the absolute right to make his own decisions. He is not a machine which turns according to God's will. He has his own faculty of deliberation. He can choose to obey God's will, or he can choose to oppose God's will and to follow the Devil's will. According to God's arrangement, the spirit should be the highest part and should control the whole being. Yet the main part of man's personality, the will, is the soul. Man's will (soul) has the power to choose to let the spirit rule, to let the body rule, or to let the self-rule. Because the soul is so powerful, the Bible calls it "a living soul."

(Collected Works of Watchman Nee, (Set 1) VOl.12: The Spiritual Man (1), Chapter 2, by Watchman Nee).

Bettina J.D. Woodard

My Parents, Lawless People, and Schools

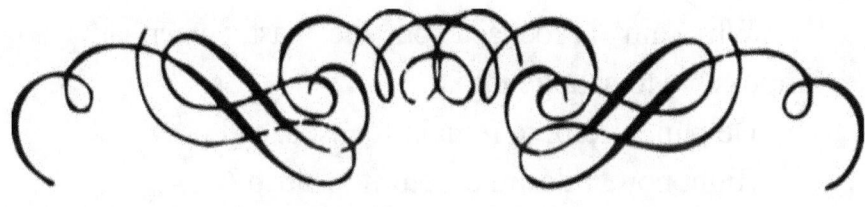

MY REARVIEW MIRROR

A myriad of thoughts and my conversation with God as I fight the urge to go back to sleep

My body refuses to go back to sleep. Perhaps God has a message for me.

I am trying to pray, but a war has been going on in my mind. As I ask for forgiveness for all my sins, my mind shifts from events that happened in the past, present, and what the future may hold for me.

Why am I focused on the past, when it is impossible to change it?

Help me, Lord, to remain focused, as I pray.

Right now, I desire to return to sleep.

Okay, the future, only God knows what is in front of me.

Lord, instruct me and others; lead us in the way we should go as you counsel us with your promises; keep your eyes on me, my family, friends, strangers, every type of leader, and enemies. Give us your wisdom and discernment so that we will know our identity, fulfill our purpose, and use our gifts according to your will. Lord, you know where we are, how we got there, and only you can rescue and deliver us from where we have strayed because of worldly glitter that was a trap set by Satan, the evil one, who cleverly used our carnal desires, as bait. Help us to forgive ourselves and others. Remove anyone being used by Satan to corrupt our finances, health,

relationships, and spirituality. Lord, help us to keep our thoughts on you, who witnessed our past, knows our present, and knows our future, instead of the circumstances in our minds where the war began. Thank you, Lord, for being our lamp and light to show us the way we should go and making provision in every area of our lives.
In the name of Jesus and by His stripes and blood. Amen.

The early morning dew still covered the windows, as I awoke by my natural time clock or was it God (my Spiritual father) who enabled me to use every faculty of my body that would be fragile and powerless, to God's storms? I tried not to give much thought to my mind's war, as I lay half asleep. I began to reminisce many misfortunes that disturbed my comfort zone and considered things that brought me joy. I realized there was something much bigger navigating my journey, allowing me the privilege of free will to make right or wrong choices.

However, the choices of yesterday were gone, tucked away and locked in the box labeled: *Forbidden*. To comfort my soul for past mistakes, I read the daily devotionals from "Today God Is First" (TGIF) and the "Holy Bible" applications that were readily available on my phone. These applications were my emotional

Band-Aids. God provided a message just for me through each Scripture and story. They were eye-opening revelations applicable to real-life situations. With these revelations, I recognized how Satan cleverly tried to recycle the same mess or steal blessings from God. Some may not agree, but choices made without God resemble the game of Russian roulette. While others may feel, praying for God's wisdom and discernment before making daily decisions, is similar to a peaceful life.

While "living forward," my uninvited memory of yesterday came to visit. I was thinking of the things that brought me joy that I felt to be blessings from God and my unpleasant past. The two were in a battle. Yesterday's memory that was secretly tucked away, a scene of childhood and my alter ego, "Super-girl Sally" were trying to dominate my mind. As I remembered how God helped me, the memory of yesterday returned forcibly like the seasons. Every experience was labeled pleasant, unpleasant, and downright ugly.

I recalled the beautiful, natural foliage of the landscaping that added appeal to the mountains of my old childhood neighborhood. It was a kind of beauty that embraced and camouflaged the area, which hid the darkness cleverly. Before getting out of bed, I glanced back at how God was present in my life; even though,

I desired the beauty of a good night's sleep, which was coming to an end.

Amazingly, when I was a child, I fell out of a tree but did not break any bones. There was another instance when my sister, our cousin, and me, were riding in the back of my father's black pickup truck, allowing the wind to freely blow through our hair and press against our eyes, as he drove us up and around the scenic view of the mountain. Without explanation, my father made everyone move to the cabin of the pickup truck, as he was pumping gas at a quick stop store. I wanted to ride in the back of the pickup, but my father insisted that I ride inside the cab of the truck. Shortly afterward, we were in an accident on the mountain, which left one wheel of the truck hanging off the side of the mountain. The police and a rescue team came to our help. If I had continued riding in the bed of the truck, I could have been seriously hurt. Another equally important incident in my life was when my older sister was babysitting me, and I became very ill. Being a child herself, she felt helpless and used her only mode of contact, running to my mother's job, while my brother watched me. My mother rushed home from work, called a cab, and placed my lifeless body on the passenger side of the cab. The driver drove as fast as he could to get me to the hospital. The doctor stated, if I had arrived any later, I would have gone into shock.

Without a doubt, God was present helping me and others not to be physically harmed.

Then there was a time one of my daughters became very ill as a young child. Although my relationship with God was not strong and I did not know His promises, I used prayer, faith, and ongoing communication with the medical team. Miraculously, we went from having all the wrong doctors to the right specialist to treat my daughter, and she regained her health. Once again, without a doubt, I believed God had orchestrated every situation so everything could happen according to His plans, without having to use anyone's manipulation. In other words, everyone had a role to fulfill just to keep me and others from great harm. God's amazing grace was ever present. God is omniscient, omnipresent, and omnipotent. I believe, and people often say, "God is always on time."

- Omniscient: God is all-knowing.
- Omnipresent: God is everywhere, at the same time.
- Omnipotent: God can do anything.

I am very thankful for the seasonal people in my life, especially those who were there while I endured many unexplainable adversities. God allowed new people to parade into my life, to encourage me, and when their time was up, they moved on to the next assignment.

As I traveled through the valleys of hurt, rejection, fear, uncertainty, pride, shame, divorce, and freedom there were times I felt alone, but God's invisible hand was there to comfort me. Because of Him, I was able to keep pressing forward even though my mind desired to look back at the forbidden zone, called *yesterday*. Sadly, I felt trapped by invisible bars of an incarcerated mind determined to travel backward in search of the promises of God.

Reflection:
Date:
Time:

BARS

Reflection:
Date:
Time:

_____
_____
_____
_____
_____
_____
_____
_____
_____
_____
_____
_____
_____

HURT

The pain of divorce leaves bruised emotions.

I had a new shame: *divorce,* to accompany many other shames. It was similar to the first shame. Once again, the emotional violation had found me. Someone I trusted and loved bruised my emotions and broke my heart. I did not understand why my story, as a married woman, was being discontinued. It would take God, to answer that question. This new label, *divorced,* was not welcomed. Giving up on life was more appealing, which led to depression, anxiety attacks, sleep apnea, and blood pressure issues. Like some women and men, because my youth was depreciating, I felt the need to try to have a procedure done to make my skin smooth like in my youth, instead, my face was left with burn spots done by a company selling a lie.

All of my side effects from divorce were stealing my peace and joy. The time came; I was hungry for freedom. I reached out to Almighty God through prayer, meditation, and faith. He heard my cry for help. I was set free from medication and therapy.

My hurt was unique; it belonged to me. In other words, no one could tell me how to feel or how long my wound would remain open. I was being held hostage to a marriage that lasted a little over two decades. "*Hush!*" before you pass judgment. You never know how you will respond to your bruised emotions and a broken heart. The healing could last a lifetime or less. Like most people stated, "Divorce is like death." Some have said it was worse than death because you have to learn to live without that person, even though he or she is still walking around alive, but has chosen another life with someone else.

Do not judge, and you will not be judged, Do not condemn, and you will not be condemned. Forgive, and you will be forgiven. (Luke 6:37)

What helped me get through the rejection of no longer being wanted by someone I loved a little over two decades? God delivered me from the deception that almost convinced me I was not a royal diamond. Free will opened the door to the desires of my heart, regardless of it being right or wrong. I strived to remember to seek God first with all my heart, soul, and mind. Without a doubt, I trusted God to bless me with someone who would accept my imperfections, just as I would accept his. With the faith of a mustard seed, I expected the total opposite of the lie that Satan tried to sell me. *Hallelujah!* That could come in many surprises because God does not try to please people. *Wow!* All things work together according to God's purpose. God's thoughts and ways are above humans. (Romans 8:28, Isaiah 55:9)

However, as it is written: What no eye has

> *seen, what no ear heard, and what no human mind has conceived the things God has prepared for those who love him.*
> *(1Corinthians 2:9)*

You might be thinking; there are two sides to every story. Regardless of who did what, I made the decision not to hang on to someone from whom God had freed me. No, it was not easy. It was similar to a drug addiction that would be toxic to one's health. I prayed daily for God to help me through the process. He did. Each day I gained independence until I was free. It was like that indescribable peace spoken of in the Bible.

> *The Lord is near. Do not be anxious about anything, but in every situation, by prayer and petition, with thanksgiving, present your request to God. And the peace of God, which transcends all understanding will guard your hearts and your minds in Christ Jesus.*
> *(Philippians 4:5b- 7)*

While in recovery from my divorce, I remained single for two years, to allow for healing. Eventually, I chose to move forward, without consulting God on whether my timing lined up with His timing. I prayed specifically for a particular type of companionship. When the time was perfect, I requested this man find me because of my poor choosing skills, but I was not aware if he was authentic or an imposter because that was not part of my particular prayer. With God, you must be specific, another lesson I have learned. I was told the potential suitor would come in threes.

Shopping at the "Great Store," where you can find most anything, I met the retired principal, who approached me. Though I was in a hurry to complete my shopping, curiosity took over. He was medium height, dressed down in blue jeans, looking like your average hard-working man, but his smile and words were captivating. The first words that came from his mouth were, "Hello Young Lady; you are looking quite lovely. Are you married?" He seemed super nice. During our brief conversation, I learned; he had divorced the same year as me. We exchanged phone numbers and talked a couple of times, interviewing one another, trying to figure out if we were a good fit, before dating.

Throughout our brief dating relationship, he never allowed me to open the car or truck door. This man would quickly run to open the door for me. We went on long rides in the country, rode to the lake and had long conversations, and traveled to nearby states, visiting the tourist attractions. Occasionally, he cooked a nice dinner or took me to a restaurant. After meeting some of his family, the frequency of the phone calls changed, but we still went out on dates. What killed the relationship? He wanted to date his ex-wife and me.

I had no interest in coming between any broken marriage; God may have been putting back together.

One day on my way to a birthday lunch, I unexpectedly made a quick stop at, "Thrifty Depot." I was getting out of my vehicle, and a gentleman approached me, as he was making his way to his truck. He was tall and handsome. As he looked over the rim of his glasses, he had a striking resemblance of "Malcolm X," a look of all about business. He introduced himself, as Derrick, and we chatted briefly. Before asking for my phone number, he asked if I was married, that was the determinant for me to give my phone number.

Eventually, I agreed to meet Derrick for our first date. I immediately noticed, Derrick lacked some of the specifics of my prayer request. Although he was very friendly, there was an absence of convictions, and I was blindsided by kindness, dates, and traveling. Not very long, after dating, I realized Derrick was a great actor too. His first presentation was excellent, but he had a "cussing demon," and now and then, the "lying demon" came out of hiding. For the most part, Derrick had an excuse to cover his lies and said, "Excuse me," when using profanity. After Derrick got comfortable being in my presence, he felt it was okay for us to live together, without being married. "Oh no!" I was not having that in my life because it was familiar, but I liked the glitter.

While I spent a lot of time at Derrick's house and was included in most of his exciting adventures, a still small voice reminded me of my convictions. To get my attention, all hell started to break loose, and things went wrong in my life. I took this as a sign to obey God. God knows how to get your attention. My attitude adjustment came quickly; I was not "giving up the milk, for free." I desired to be steadfast in my convictions. My opinion, fornication, though biblically wrong, it is like food and water and very similar to a strong drug addiction. The need to fornicate can cause the strongest man or woman to break their conviction to be abstinent. The glitter of kindness, dates, and traveling with Derrick was the bait Satan was using to distract me from my convictions of striving to honor Godly principles put in place for every male and female to have their own husband and wife. It was not difficult to see Derrick had been disappointed by people wearing some façade, too. Everything connected with evil deeds has a price named: *Failure*.

It was time to get out of bed, but I was being held hostage by my memory of childhood. Many thoughts were trying to take precedence, but the memory of yesterday was stealing my day. I had the power to say, *No,* to the thoughts that lied about my identity, and the plans that were predestined just for me.

It was time to go back and become free, so I took a leap of faith and launched backward in time. Going back was like a spinning merry-go-round, racing in time that allowed brief and instant replays of the pleasant, unpleasant, and downright ugly. Though painful, every dimension rehearsed began at a time between the ages of four and five and continued. It did not matter my age, who my friends were or my accomplishments.

While being incarcerated in time, I constantly asked, *Why?* Some questions were left unanswered. Even the perpetrators would not be able to reveal the answer. Do you believe every soul is constantly at war with the spirit? If that is true, can one explain the "why" for their actions? Every good and bad experience had its different season. I learned God was in control of each outcome, not worry, or manipulation.

Reflection:
Date:
Time:

BARS

Reflection:
Date:
Time:

REJECTION

"Please stop hurting me, I'm already broken!"

I slowed down while traveling backward in time so some of the events of my adversities could be revealed to the "eye of the beholder." First, I remembered former words and behaviors from those inside my childhood house. Second, the changeable entourage could be seen and heard. Third, the old neighborhood and outside beauty of my childhood house were slowly coming into focus, along with many amenities. In spite of the vivid view, I was not looking forward to what was to come. God, Jesus, and the Holy Spirit had to be helping me because I did not stop my journey, while painfully remembering others' spoken words. My emotions controlled my attitude. Some people may not be able to relate to some of my challenges of yesterday's past.

When I was made aware of what took place while being in my mother's womb, I became upset. Like many, I dwelt on negative words and experiences. My mother's statements were, "I never wanted a third child. You made me very sick. I never took vitamins; you turned out okay." Very untrue, due to poor nutrition during her pregnancy, I was born a fragile baby, who could not be around people with colds or the whooping cough. Those illnesses would have caused me death. I fought for my very existence.

Fortunately, an older lady my mother met while she was at the hospital seeking medical attention for me, advised her to take me to another hospital to get better care, if she wanted me to get well. Of course, my mother took the lady's advice. I was taken to another hospital downtown, where I received a private doctor and medical treatment. In time, under the physician's care, I grew stronger as an infant.

As a preschooler, I felt defeated, due to challenges with severe anemia. I often felt cold, and my skin cracked and bled. After suffering for a while, I was taken to the doctor. Part of my treatment plan was eating foods I hated: liver, eggs, spinach, beef, beans, greens, and beets. Though beneficial, it was like torture, for a child who was only four years old. My face cringed, as I slowly ate and attempted to regurgitate my food. While being at war with anemia, I battled flaking, itching, and cracking skin.

Even more significant, was my changeable entourage of friends in the neighborhood who taunted me, making me feel so antagonized. I wanted to punch those, "friend/enemies." Eventually, anemia was annihilated, through proper nutrition.

Perhaps, I was extra sensitive to information my mother should have kept private. My mother, Sue, was not very tactful. She was blunt. If I seemed weak, Sue used her remedy to make me strong. She had the attitude, if it does not bother her, then it should not bother anyone. People are unique, for some, "Time heals all wounds," for others, wounds still hurt in spite of time. I wanted my mother's comfort. The negative words spoken by Sue may have been meaningless, but those words were hurtful. I reached the point of not complaining to Sue. It felt better to internalize the hurt. Emotionally, I wanted to scream: *Please stop hurting me, I am already broken!* Friends and family were breaking me, emotionally. I felt ignored because no one seemed to acknowledge the agony that was attacking me. The words Sue echoed over and over again, and I told myself, *Ignore them!*

Even though the memory caused my eyes to fill with tears, I disregarded my emotions and continued the road trip backward. I journeyed to a remote place in my mind and began to daydream of a time when I should have had a life filled with normalcy. According to my dreams, I desired a life like the old wholesome TV families of the 1960's: a family unit that was free of division and confusion, people that loved one another and were quick to problem-solve, and a happy ending every time, regardless of the chaos. At times, I found myself in a place of nothingness because of the piercing comments made by those I loved and liked.

Words can build up or tear someone down. How would you feel if your parent shared, you were an unwanted pregnancy? Unfortunately, I was not aware that my emotions were very much like a car gauge that warns when overheating is happening. Although my emotions were an indication of where Satan was attacking me, there was no knowledge of God's promises to fight the battle that was going on in my mind.

As a child between four and five years old, the significance of God was not known. I slept during church, and whatever the message was about, there was no reinforcement at home. Since I was dealing with the "battle of the mind," I medicated my troubles by hanging out with my "friend/enemies." The comradery was necessary. They were the other people that made me happy and sad, in the lawless neighborhood, where I was entertained by all types of grown-up drama.

At home, I felt like an only child. Whenever I was alone with my older sister, she pretended to be a scary critter or a killer with a knife. I would run to the nearest neighbor's house for refuge. I reported her actions to Sue and her response was, "The girl just foolish." This behavior made me frantic. Quite often, my older sister avoided me as much as possible. She rarely talked to me. She was very involved with her peers and extracurricular school activities. Sue used me as a form of contraceptive to prevent my older sister from being along with boys. My older sister could not attend any of the school events, unless, she was "chaperoned" by me, her little sister. My sister was very busy as she journeyed through school. And Sue kept her oldest daughter busy helping out with some of the chores at home, such as, cooking, cleaning, and babysitting her brother and me. If time allowed, Sue permitted her oldest daughter to sew, on a sewing machine. Maybe my sister resented me, even though I was not the one putting grown-up responsibilities on her.

My brother was cool; I regarded him as a friend. He spent a lot of time hanging out with his buddies, doing typical boy stuff. Sometimes, they allowed me to join them so I could learn how to defend myself physically. Unfortunately, as my brother grew older, he suffered a nervous breakdown and was institutionalized. He lived at home, part-time. I was bewildered about what had taken place in his life. I could not understand the monumental shift of events that changed his paradigm. I loved my brother, but could not recognize him as the person I used to know.

For a season in time, he was like the average person, full of life. One day, without foreseen warning, some unknown evil stole his normalcy. As he aged, illness suddenly came and took his life. There was no human explanation for what happened to my brother's life, but it was a reminder of how life can be short, and anything can change at any given time.

There is a time for everything, and a season for every activity under the heavens: a time to be born and a time to die, a time to plant and a time to uproot, a time to kill and a time to heal, a time to tear down and a time to build, a time to weep and a time to laugh, a time to mourn and a time to dance, a time to scatter stones and a time to gather them, a time to embrace and to refrain from embracing, a time to search and a time to give up, a time to keep and a time to throw away, a time to mend, a time to be silent and a time to speak, a time to love and a time to hate, a time for war and a time for peace. (Ecclesiastes 3:1-8)

During the 1960's, not many people drove through my old neighborhood, Helltown, located at the foot of the mountain, because it was very isolated and off the main route, leading to the mountain. One would have to purposely leave the main road to experience the outward beauty of this small community. It was a sight of beauty, although the citizens and neighbors in the community were unruly. Like that old cliché, "You cannot judge a book by its cover."

On days when the streets were empty without distractions of the contentious people breaking some law, it was possible to notice the beauty of the surrounding mountains and all the conveniences available for the people. Helltown was a community that consisted of people that lacked morals and standards. The people carried their anger on their faces. Most of the people never smiled but seemed to get pleasure by frowning. When some of the adults got angry, they used some weapon of destruction to problem-solve, such as, condemning words, guns, knives, or fighting towards death, then they called the law. Many were convicted and executed by the hands of someone they knew in the community.

What made the community attractive? Helltown was mostly populated by one type of people; I would describe as lawless. It was sheltered by beautiful mountains and seasonal weather, convenient stores, a hotel, drive-in movie theater, daycare, and major grocery store, which made it possible for the people to walk to purchase supplies.

In the spring, children would fill the streets to play ball, ride bikes, play made up street games, and enjoy the neighborhood playground. The daycare that my friends and I attended was adjacent to the playground. On occasion, adults would be seen on the playground socializing too. When winter arrived, the streets were void of life.

In spite of the beauty that camouflaged the darkness, like me, most of the kids did not have positive role models to demonstrate how to respect others. Therefore, I did not have a strong desire to have others in my life. I tolerated my friends' changeable attitudes. They constantly teased one another about their flaws. The group had no respect for differences. That made it difficult just to have fun, so I felt like an outcast. Negative words and experiences took root in my mind. The spirit of rejection, fear, a lack of courage and confidence were birthed in me. I was unaware of the Scripture that said,

> *For the Spirit God gave us does not make us timid, but gives us power, love and self-discipline. (2 Timothy 1:7)*

Although I attended church with Sue, my siblings and I slept during the service. Sometimes I visited the church near my childhood home located across the street from where I lived. No one acknowledged that the kids needed to be taught on a different level to increase their understanding. The church was viewed negatively because grown people cried, yelled in a foreign language, and ran up and down the aisle. And I was forced to attend a place where people appeared sad, the day before school, on Monday.

The school was my happy place, however, being born in a family and a part of a neighborhood full of deprivation, I could not dodge being stereotyped as a by-product of the underprivileged adults and children.

The children were my entourage that changed daily. The reviews that came from them were critical, uncritical, and enthusiastic. I seldom played with the same friends because I was an adventurous little girl that enjoyed the company of others, although, typically quiet. My changeable entourage, brought out, "Super-girl Sally," my alter ego, who was always on fire for adventure. "Super-girl Sally" was not shy, quiet, and fearful. She was free from any inhibitions restricting her from exploring the unknown.

Reflection:
Date:
Time:

BARS

Reflection:
Date:
Time:

_____

_____

_____

_____

_____

_____

_____

_____

_____

_____

_____

_____

_____

FEAR

I suffered from the whiplash of the past.

BARS

In the neighborhood, most of my friends lived in a home with a father and mother. It was a bittersweet environment, clothed in grief. Not only was my home infested with secrets and lies; the infestation was a pandemic in the homes of my entourage. Open abuse was rapid. Mothers and fathers in the neighborhood, sadly, had no shame for their infidelity. It was heavily practiced. In my eyes, it appeared to be, "tit for tat." It was typical for the neighborhood married men to have open relationships with other single or married women in the small community that sat behind a major grocery store.

There were two churches in this area and yet, all kinds of evil took place in my house and the other houses in the community. The drama took place daily, in the circle of the small brick-and-mortar houses that were connected to one another. Every type of harmful exposure was going on, which included children between the ages of 12 and 15 having children. It became normal for me and the changeable entourage of friends to be on the playground, at the daycare after hours, enjoying unsupervised play time. From the playground, we witnessed horrible abuse; women were physically beaten in the street, phone booth, and in front of the grocery store. Derogatory language was used and referenced women as bitches, whores, and cocksuckers. Men were shot or stabbed for unknown reasons. The drama had no respect for those of us who were between the ages of four and six. Sadly, there was no therapeutic help offered, during that time. We had to develop a tough skin.

As the years passed, the people of the neighborhood that caused most of the drama died due to illness or brutality at the hands of one another. Secretly, all of the childhood trauma was tucked inside of my mental Pandora's Box. I kept it hidden by my pretentious ways; as I transitioned to new environments and relationships. Left behind were insecurities that were so ingrained that my validations were only recognized when it came from others.

Invalidation began in the A-framed house that sat on "Confusion Avenue," where I lived. The A-framed house was practical and surrounded by hedges. It housed a typical size family. On the outside, it was well manicured. The inside reflected the lawless neighborhood. Not by choice but by chance, I got the privilege to learn how to be a parent and an adult from my parents and the community people. Our house was like a cage, which caused me to be very quiet and restrain my personality.

Contrarily, when I met with my entourage, "Super-girl Sally," my alter ego came to life. She was full of adventure and a risk taker. As I matured into a young woman, my character displayed my first audience, as the seasons of life brought many adventures.

At different episodes in my life, I would get distracted by pleasant experiences, while the unpleasant scene of childhood was dormant and unexpectedly waiting to appear. The journey filled with ups and downs seemed to last forever. Many experiences were like a wound that would not heal. Some memories would re-puncture the emotional bruises like an ice pick, chipping away old ice. My memories were similar to nature's seasons, forcing their way back in, without warning, even when the emotional climate was at peace. There was no awareness of the sovereignty of God who allows us to dwell in the secret place of the Most High and rest because He stands between us and anything that creates havoc in our lives.

Since I slept during church service, there was no awareness of God's many names and promises. His invisible hand had to be there. Only God could have preserved me as I journeyed through life, encountering perverted evil, falling into the pit and remaining in the hole for a season. Every decision was made without wisdom; even though, God would have given wisdom to me abundantly, daily, if I had asked concerning any area of my life.

If any of you lacks wisdom, you should ask God, who gives generously to all without

finding fault, and it will be given to you."
(James 1:5)

God's names uncover His personality and nature. Some of God's names are "Jehovah-Jireh, our Provider; Jehovah-Shalom, our Peace; Elohim, the strong, making a way for you out of no way; Jehovah-Nissi, the Lord my Banner; Jehovah-Rapha, the Lord that heals; Jehovah-Shammah, the Lord is there."

As a result of being betrayed by those loved and liked, resentment brought with it anger, bitterness, hate, and unforgiveness. The emotional baggage was like a disease that required a specialist in emotional reconstruction, to cure it. I desired normalcy, but how would I know what that looked or felt like if never experienced it? There was an old expression often quoted by the elderly, "Children live what they learn," and that was very true for me. I say "kudos" to me; I was very skilled on how to parade a façade.

Harry and Sue demonstrated exceptionally well, poor character examples. Harry was selfish, uncaring, and disrespectful towards his wife and children. In front of others, he was a great provider because he kept a roof over his family's head. He spent time with his kids, gave to his needy less fortunate friends. He even shared family outings with some of the kids in the neighborhood and was always willing to share a meal with others, even if he had to give up his portion of food.

On the other hand, Sue showed weakness. It did not matter what Harry was doing to disrespect her; Sue was quick to forgive. When Harry openly committed adultery, these two would argue and physically fight and later continued as if nothing ever happened. During their many years of marriage, I never heard either one of them say the words, *I love you* or express love. It was like a combat zone. Randomly, the war would take place, and Sue always gave a truce to be kind, respectful and kept integrity in the marriage. I was left in the dark, never learning how to love myself and demand respect from others.

The A-framed house on "Confusion Lane" was no "Alice in Wonderland," where the vivid view of my rearview mirror began. As bleak as it may sound, unknowingly, "Judas" showed up in my life early, while at a vulnerable age when you depend on adults for safety. Sooner or later, "Judas" clothed himself or herself in many disguises to negate what God would have for the future. As mind-blowing as it may seem, every experience, though pleasant, unpleasant, and the downright ugly, left me with seeds of good and evil that blossomed into teaching, strengthening, healing, and restoring.

The past experiences that left seeds of defeat could have caused me to be isolated from others and hindered me from succeeding in school. Instead, I kept on enjoying my friends and loving school. Though I suffered from the whiplash of the past, I had been told; *You must live forward.* Contrarily, looking backward, helped me to live forward and reflect on how God was present and protected me in every experience. Even, God has warned us not to look back. According to this Scripture,

> *Jesus replied, No one who puts a hand to the plow and looks back is fit for the kingdom of God. (Luke 9:62)*

Reflection:
Date:
Time:

BARS

Reflection:
Date:
Time:

UNCERTAINTY

My quietness was a place of quiet storms.

Sue was full-figured, short, and anti-sociable. She was known for her bedroom eyes and plump jaws that indicated her love for cooking. Sue faithfully maintained her hairstyle by frequently visiting the beauty shop, using money left over from the family's budget. Sue prepared all week to make sure she was fully coordinated from head to toe, making sure to incorporate some bling into her outfit, to be ready for church on Sunday. Sue perceived the people in the church, as decent and respectful. While on the other hand, the people in the neighborhood were seen as heathens, she avoided.

Communication was not Sue's strength, nor was it encouraged in the family between the siblings or the parents, so secrets were easily kept. The kitchen, during meal-times, provided the best opportunity for communication. Conversations about achievements, future careers or appropriate sexual boundaries, were avoided. Though the family rarely talked, Sue shared about her childhood and how great of a man her father was. Some of her comments were, "He was strong, loving, and he treated my mother well." On the other hand, Sue's mother was a busybody. She was known for talking about neighborly women and was corrected by Sue's father who did not believe in that kind of nonsense. Maybe Sue was replicating her father who only talked when correction was necessary.

Sue could not remember a time when her father was not working on the farm to make sure his family's needs were met. Both parents were very skillful in canning and stretching their food. Sue's mother and father were sharecroppers. Sue shared the same talent on how to stretch the food and money. Sue's physical appearance demonstrated her first love for style, food, and stretching the money.

Sue's second love was taking care of her children and her husband, Harry, regardless of his actions. Her third love was going to church. Sue always insisted on taking my siblings and me. The preacher's sermon would always put the children to sleep. Sue would spend the entire service telling us to sit up and stay awake. As we approached the teen years, Sue stopped trying so hard to make us attend church because we were getting certificates from school for learning Scriptures. After church, Sue prepared Harry some of her home cooking. She cooked on Saturdays, for the Sunday meal. Sue was a good cook; she managed her kitchen like a school cafeteria. Each day had its special menu. Everyone sat at the kitchen table, except Harry. He ate wherever he chose. Although mealtime was the opportunity for conversation, we were rushed to finish our meal so the kitchen could be cleaned.

During the week, while the house was empty, Sue would indulge in the soap operas. Her favorites were:

General Hospital, All My Children, Young and the Restless, and Days of Our Lives.

When Sue did talk, it would be something about the soaps. She should have used her time more constructively and learned a new skill. To end Sue's transportation dependency on Harry, taxi cabs, and buses, she could have learned how to drive instead of watching the soaps. Although gas and alternative transportation were cheap, during that era, having the skill to drive would have been priceless. On occasion, Harry drove Sue to various destinations. Most of the time, Sue caught a cab or the city bus to her destinations. Her choices were based on where she was going. If she was going to church, she used a cab. To shop for clothes she took the city bus, however, this rarely happened since she did not like to walk too far.

Even though the grocery store was only a short block away, Sue had me, only five years old, walk to get grocery items. She trusted her five-year-old daughter with the responsibility of grocery shopping for a few things. I was handed a twenty dollar bill and a list. Sue always said, "Go straight to the store and come straight back." It was scary walking to the store. I had to dodge many cars and delivery trucks.

When I reached the store, I browsed each section of the store, especially the toy section, which made the experience better and not so horrific. After I had gathered all the groceries, I handed the money to the cashier. She placed the change and receipt inside the bag and echoed the same words, "Go straight home."

One day while I was at the grocery store, I noticed a pair of high heel shoes in the toy section. Oh, how I longed to have those shoes. I shared the desire to have those shoes with my mother, Sue, who avoided communication unless it was about a soap opera character or how great her father was. The interest was ignored, so I began to plot on how to get the money from Sue's handbag, to obtain the shoes. The obsession with having the shoes, haunted my mind day and night, at the daycare, and while hanging out with the changeable entourage. The shoes became a part of my dreams. I tried very hard to practice patience and wait for Sue to oblige. At the same time, Sue worked hard to avoid communicating to help me alleviate the obsession.

Then the unthinkable happened, one day the opportunity came, just like a gift and I seized it. While Sue was busy cooking and watching all of her favorite soap operas, her handbag was violated. A twenty-dollar bill was stolen. I used my limitless freedom and walked to the grocery store to purchase my high heels. As usual, the cashier placed the change inside of the bag and stated, "Go straight home." Upon arriving at home, the new high heels were paraded around in front of Sue and the other family members. Sue was finally communicating. She asked how the shoes were purchased; the truth was revealed. The money confiscated from Sue's bag was admitted by the perpetrator, me. Sue used the feared razor belt to whip, scorn, and correct me. After I calmed down, Sue escorted me to the grocery store to return the high heel shoes. The cashier commented, "I knew something was not right with her having twenty dollars to purchase those shoes." I learned that stealing caused brutal pain, and Sue finally walked to the store that was less than a block away but failed to see how she missed the opportunity to teach me the importance of listening, communicating, and problem-solving.

Who was Harry? He had beady eyes that indicated sneakiness, straight black hair, a strong jawline, a short athletic build with a full midsection. Harry got his exercise from spending a lot of time running around in the streets, and frequently visiting the "good time houses," where he would perpetrate being financially successful to those less fortunate than he was.

Harry was known for being a family man, who worked two jobs to pay the bills because he had chosen for Sue to stay home or work only part-time. Harry believed a woman's place was to be at home to cook, clean, and be available for wifely duties to her husband. Also, he was known for using the heavy-duty leather strap on his kids, if needed.

Whenever others were visiting the home, Harry had a strong habit of exaggerating the truth. Some of his lies included being an army veteran, a gun collector, and having enough money to share with his less fortunate friends and begging relatives, in spite of the hardship it caused the family. Harry seemed reasonable on the outside, a father who was hard working that was doing his best to meet the needs of the family. His wife, Sue was a stay-at-home mother that only financially contributed when permitted by Harry. Sue was allowed by Harry to work at the daycare across the street from the house part-time. I was permitted to attend the daycare part-time too. Sue and I were not at the daycare, at the same time.

The daycare playground was where I became "Super-girl Sally." The metamorphosis would take place immediately. As soon as the changeable entourage would meet, "Super-girl Sally" and her entourage would exchange words and do tricks on the playground equipment. Sometimes, someone in the group would bring a turntable that operated by batteries. Sally and her friends would dance, talk about boys in the neighborhood, and school. Sally was always happy to meet up with her entourage because it was a way to escape her home life. Whenever Sally attended daycare, she would once again become very quiet and convert back to being me. Often, the teachers would ask,

Sue, why I was so quiet. Sue would reply, "She has always been that way, very quiet."

My quietness was a place of quiet storms that came into existence when innocence and confusion crossed paths.

Some events happened in Sue's life that troubled me. For instance when Sue was in an institution for her nerves. I did not know why Sue had experienced that type of therapy. I never forgot the incident when Sue and I were on the public transportation coming from downtown, and she began to act differently. Sue cried and repeatedly stated, "I am so nervous." An older lady was on the bus that day, whipped out what was referred to as the "spirit of ammonia." After Sue had inhaled the substance in the small bottle, she calmed down, to almost normal. I was a young child, my heart was sad, and I felt Sue was a very broken woman. I knew in my tender heart, Harry, "who was lower than a snake," had something to do with it. Harry's façade: he was good to others, outside the home, but in the privacy of his home, he was disrespectful.

He was known for having a keen interest in young women. Harry was so disrespectful that he would bring women inside of Sue's home. Sue and his children openly witnessed him driving women around in one of his vehicles. Harry knew how to repair vehicles and fix things around the house. He was a "jack of all trades," he was very handy around the house, in spite of his very messy ways.

Some of Harry's behaviors were very dark. My sister had some of her friends visiting from the neighborhood. Harry was laying on the couch in his boxer shorts, pretending to be asleep. One of the girls went to the restroom. After time had passed, the other girls and I caught the missing girl sitting on top of Harry, while he only had on boxer shorts. Because of Harry's ways, I became desensitized to love and trust. My experiences of pain grew, and the events were again, hidden inside my mental Pandora's Box. I kept it locked for many years. The wounds of yesterday always interrupted my day. I wanted to be transparent and tell someone, but I felt no one would believe me.

Harry had this great reputation for always helping others. He especially took an interest in children. Obviously, Harry was an undercover pedophile that others seemed to overlook. Sadly, although Harry drank alcohol heavily, smoked, and gambled, he was a pillar of the lawless community and deeply loved by his siblings and Sue's family. The people of the neighborhood trusted him. Maybe Harry was trusted because he appeared so noble to his children. He made sure others saw him teaching his kids how to drive at a very early age. Also, along with his children, Harry would gather up the neighborhood's children, give them a ride to school, take them to the amusement park, and take them swimming at one of the community centers. He was always willing to feed and provide liquor to his acquaintances. Harry was known for being charitable by giving others money but privately complained to Sue. It was like Harry was trying to make up for his evil deeds in an unorthodox way.

Was Sue blamed for what happened? No. I secretly hated Harry. Every day, my peace was robbed and haunted by what he did to me. Be mindful; I was between four and five years of age. I carried that secret from early childhood to puberty, from adolescence to adulthood. The easy way out was being silent to protect what appeared to be stability for the family, to friends and relatives, while becoming a hostage to my dark secret. I was protecting the idea of stability because there was no awareness of what that looked like. I only knew what I learned from the exposure of my childhood home life and the lawless neighborhood.

As maturity crept upon me, I often wondered if I had been fair to Sue who deserved a better companion. Many could have their best answer. Remember, I was only between four and five years of age, trying to cope with misunderstood experiences.

My alter ego, "Super-girl Sally" was my only way of mental escape. As I hung out with my friends, I used my limitless freedom to leave the playground and venture miles away from what was supposed to be the safety of home. At times, while Sally and her friends were walking in the neighborhood, along the avenue, Caucasian men would speed by in their vehicles, trying to run over us, yelling, *"Niggers."* Sally and her entourage would scatter. Their adrenalin would be pumped up over the experience, but it would not stop Sally and her friends from walking along the avenue and allow their impulsiveness to sway them to walk to the nearest projects or cross major, dangerous streets to get to the foot of the mountain where some of the other friends lived. These friends were only seen at school. In those days parents would say, "Be home when the street lights come on." There was so much time for mischief.

At times, the boys in the neighborhood would meet up with Sally and some of her friends to play house in abandoned houses. Someone would pretend to be the father, mother, and children. Discarded items that were in the abandoned house would be used to portray being a grown-up and taking care of the family. This included having pretend sex while being dressed, but acting out the body movements.

Sally had not learned boundaries. Like most of the neighborhood homes, the Sally that lived in me shared living in a dysfunctional house. My façade was, I had a family that was good, but behind closed doors, cleverly hidden, was a little girl who was wounded by her secret shame.

> *For I know the plans I have for you, declares*
> *the Lord, plans to prosper you and not harm*
> *you, plans to give you hope and future.*
> *Jeremiah 29:11*

Reflection:
Date:
Time:

BARS

Reflection:
Date:
Time:

PRIDE

School seemed to be a haven.

Elementary school

School was a way to escape from the issues of home and community. No one knew I was carrying baggage from my home and neighborhood that was camouflaged by my sweet personality. During that season of life, I was young and did not quite understand my trauma, but knew how to use charisma and charm. People were drawn to me, but I did not know how to receive others, due to a lack of trust. One of my skills I learned from home was how to perpetrate being something that I was not.

My first day at Pride Elementary was effortless because I was a great actress. I viewed it as a home away from home because of the loving environment. The teachers greeted each child, as he or she entered the classroom. Being greeted made me feel special. Getting up and getting ready for school was easy and very much enjoyed. The two-level red building was old, with cracked sheetrock walls and a basement that housed some of the restrooms. I fondly recall the smell of the old building that needed a facelift or needed to be demolished and walking to the cafeteria where all the food was delicious, with the expectations of sitting with chosen friends. I was at school every day unless I was sick. During that era, kids had to have celebrated their sixth birthday before September 21 to enter the first grade. Elementary school was from first grade to sixth grade.

In spite of being very young, the neighborhood kids would start out walking to school in the mornings and hopefully catch up with one of their neighborhood buddies to make the dangerous walk to school, crossing a major highway, would be less fearful. Depending on daylight savings time, it could be dark. That journey could include witnessing an unsupervised kid being hit by a moving car, watching the helpless child lay on the concrete until medical help and the police arrived. Regardless of the treacherous journey, "Back in the Day," the school seemed to be a haven for the kids that parents could trust. However, the journey to get there was very unsafe. It resembled Russian roulette; it was lethal.

What was important to me beyond the musky smell of the old school building? I looked forward to seeing my entourage of friends in one place. Although structured, the classroom, lunchtime, and recess allowed extra time to congregate, which gave me time to become "Super-girl Sally" briefly. As the day began, homework was first on the agenda to be collected; I was always prepared. No one ever had to remind me to do homework. Notoriety was critical. I loved it when the teachers would brag about me for being successful. When a teacher called on me for questions, I usually knew the answers. I was frequently bragged about to my mother, Sue. That caused me to smile and walk proudly. I did not know why, but Bible class was my favorite too.

A lady would come on an assigned day to the elementary school, to teach Bible verses to kids who were interested in learning and had permission forms from their parents. I loved that class which was located in a secluded room. I especially enjoyed receiving a certificate for learning the assigned Scriptures. Since there was no reinforcement at home, sadly, I did not get the significance of learning and remembering Scriptures and how I could have used those Scriptures to fight the battles of my mind. There was learning without retaining the full coat of armor of God's inspired Word. At home, no one asked me about the Bible Scriptures that we discussed at school. Unfortunately for me, the Bible class was just another part of the school's extracurricular activities. In addition to loving Bible, I enjoyed the holidays and participating in plays to enhance my acting skills.

During the school year, holidays were celebrated with a party or some event in the auditorium. If there was a play, I tried out for a speaking part. No one detected what was in my mental Pandora's Box. Inside the walls of the school, there was no sign of problems at home.

After school, my routine each day was to come

back home and complete my homework quickly so I could leave the house to hang out with my changeable entourage of friends. I was generous with sharing my intelligence with the neighborhood kids. If I went to one of my friend's house and their homework was not done, I offered my assistance to complete any assignments, so that we could hang out before curfew. The street lights were our signal when it was time to return home.

Junior High School

Junior High school was an old red brick building with three floors that had walls with cracks and blemishes. The school had an excellent staff that recognized each child, as being special. Some of the changeable entourage of friends had thinned out, due to uncontrollable circumstances, but that was okay. The condition of the school had not changed, compared to the former elementary school. In other words, the building was old with a musty smell that needed to be updated or demolished. In addition to what continued, my remaining friends and I from the neighborhood had to journey across a major highway to get to the school. The highway did not have a red light to slow down the traffic. It was scary; the vehicles would speed by dodging the children, who were trying to avoid getting hit. Unfortunately, there were no buses to conveniently take us to school and drop us off at the front entrance. Sometimes, in the winter months, on cold days the parents took turns driving the kids to school. What was bad about that? Most of the parents smoked cigarettes with the car windows rolled up, while driving the kids to school.

Every day, I walked alone or with friends, and passed a funeral home to get to school, which was very eerie. On occasion, while crossing the street to get to school, my friends and I would witness one of the children from the neighborhood being savagely hit by a moving car. Afterwards, we watched a helpless child lying in the street like road kill, waiting for the police and ambulance. The next day, life continued, as if nothing happened. In other words, we continued to walk to school trampling through dangerous territory and after we had got to school, no one seemed to care about how witnessing a child getting hit by a moving car could have impacted our mental state. There was no counseling offered. You would think the horrific scenery would have caused us to become desensitized. It caused me to have catastrophic thoughts. Eventually, a crossing guard was assigned to help the kids cross the street.

Of course, life had to keep moving; it did not matter about being bewildered by the drama. I was about to encounter new friends and teachers. Once acclimated to the new school, I excelled. One of my favorite extra-curricular activities was Bible, but they did not offer it at the new school. Other than the Bible teacher, no one told me the significance of memorizing Scriptures. Without a clear understanding, I felt calm and at peace during my Bible classes and loved receiving certificates. My gift for remembering information was rewarding me with accolades. Though the Bible class was just another way to earn an award, I was also hungry for approval from people.

Just like in elementary school, without failure, my assignments were always completed and turned in on time. The only time I was absent, was due to sickness. Though I had grown up in a segregated neighborhood, now the entourage of friends was changing to a diverse group of friends in school. They lived closer to the mountain. Their cultural differences did not create barriers to relationship building. My new female friends would talk about how they discussed planning their weddings in the eighth and ninth grades and their future careers with their parents. Unfortunately, some of my young female friends in the neighborhood dropped out of school because of unplanned pregnancies. No one at my house was having those types of conversations; all I had to share was my mother's famous phrase, "Don't *brang* no baby in this house!" which was often echoed. No one sat around the kitchen table or in a family room to discuss the future. When Sue talked, it was still about the soap operas and her daddy, who was a good man.

In spite of different family traditions, my new friends of another race and I connected at school. Camaraderie was developed between us too but only lasted for three years. After middle school, our contact discontinued. I was zoned to a segregated high school because the school district was claiming to create racial balance to create equal education for all students.

As the years passed, the neighborhood entourage changed due to people moving out of the neighborhood, and many of the memorized Scriptures were forgotten that once gave me a sense of calmness and peace. Although I adored the Bible teacher, each Scripture was God's promise that was replacing my negative thought. In other words, each Scripture was medicine for the battle that was attacking my mind. Like most learning, "If you do not use it, you will lose it." According to Scripture,

> *...turn your ear to my words. Do not let them out of your sight, keep them within your heart; for they are life to those who find them and health to one's whole body, above all guard your heart, for everything you do flows from*

it. (Proverbs 4:20-23)

High School

High school was a musky damp smelling, large red brick building with three floors of much-needed renovation built in 1865. It needed to be demolished. There were no teachers to greet you on the first day. Now, my entourage of friends had gotten even smaller. They could be counted on one hand. Most of my friends had moved to other areas of the city or another state. This school was not my choice to attend. To remain connected to diverse friends from middle school, my choice was a school located downtown. In spite of the changes in the dynamics of what was familiar to me, I embraced my unseen future at the high school. I was very cautious and used very limited words. I was only open to relationships with students that I encountered in my classes and avoided extracurricular activities. The fear of rejection was anticipated and would somehow find me.

As I progressed in school, going from the tenth grade to the twelfth grade, there were teachers I liked, and some I preferred not to encounter. Though quiet, I was well liked by peers. Some of the girls would say, "She respects other people's men; she is cool." For some, when dating took place in the high school, it accompanied ownership of another person. I was very careful not step on anyone's toes. The girls or guys would fight if someone was trying to show some interest in whom he or she was dating. The girls were going as far as having a baby or children by guys they were dating in high school. In spite of their naive choices, a lot of the students were successful academically, including me.

One day while I was in the company of my peers, it was suggested that I run for Ms. Pride High School Queen. Regretfully, I did not have nice clothes to wear, like my sister did when she attended the same school and who came in third place for the best dresser. In pursuit of my pipe dreams, I began the necessary steps to be accepted in a position of royalty. Everything was in check. I had excellent grades and no behavior issues.

My strategy, there was no need for me to do anything but continue being respectful and I would continue to be liked. My only other requirement was that I maintained my "B" average. Unfortunately, I had a "Judas," among the teacher's faculty. The Vocational Business Education, VBE, teacher called me to a private meeting after class and stated to me, "I have been made aware, you are running for Ms. Pride. You would not represent the school very well. You need to withdraw." I was heart-broken and shed tears. There was no indication this teacher felt like this towards me.

This teacher began to sabotage me by lowering my grade, just enough to keep me from being able to run for Ms. Pride. My effort to succeed in VBE was effortless. The spirit of rejection had found me in an authority figure that I respected. Mysteriously, after I withdrew as a candidate for Ms. Pride, my grades improved to a "B" average again. I never looked at that teacher the same again.

After that negative experience with the VBE teacher, like most typical high schoolers, I started secretly dating a guy two years older. I was a junior, and he was a senior, ready to graduate. He lived in one of the projects known for violence. This guy was nice in the beginning.

As the relationship accumulated time, he began to show his crazy side of possessiveness. He did not want me around my cousin, who was like a sister or anyone else, but him. While attending a basketball game, he and I had a physical fight. Remember, my brother and his friends had taught me how to defend myself physically, so he remembered that rumble. We had to leave the game because of the disturbance we were causing. The walk to the car was like that of a cat, silent, but ready to attack. He drove very slowly taking me home as if he was plotting something sinister. You could feel his anger. Suddenly, he stopped at a graveyard and tried to pull me out of his car. Although I was frightened, I was thinking. The car's engine was running, as he sought to pull me from the driver side of the car. Since he was not successful, he went to the passenger's side. As he ran around the car, I hurried to the driver's side and drove off, leaving dust on his face. That was a horrific experience, and I broke off that relationship that night when he came to my parent's house to get his car. I felt some powerful force had been protecting me. After that relationship, I took a break from dating and began to think about my future. I had no idea what career path to choose, my interest in high school was business. Because of a lack of confidence, there was always uncertainty brewing in my brain.

    On the way to obtaining new accolades of life, there were many evil forces rooted in from childhood. While twilighting, the school experiences of elementary, junior high, and high school were sweet and bitter memories. My goal was not to be "the product of the environment." The odds of being successful were strenuous. I desired just to be accepted, without being an overachiever. The sweetest years were in elementary, where love and acceptance were felt, by teachers. Middle school was great. I loved having diverse relationships with Caucasian and African-American friends. Home economics class was my favorite class. We were allowed to cook simple foods from items stored in the pantry. We learned how to sew street clothes from a pattern. After making my first outfit, I received compliments. High school was very similar to my neighborhood, full of deprivation. Therefore, what I saw in my day to day life at home was being reinforced while at school. There was very little hope of avoiding the behaviors of the lawless people from the neighborhood because their children were, "living what they learned," at school.

Reflection:
Date:
Time:

BARS

Reflection:
Date:
Time:

SHAME

I was perishing on the inside.

As I tried to process life on my journey beyond high school, there was another voice that would not let me forget my first shame. My first shame, my secret that took root between four and five years of age became my first piece of mental baggage. I purposely tried to leave it behind, at different seasons of my life, but it refused to leave. Remember, I had not been taught how to respect anything or anyone, but I knew how to keep secrets. That old cliché, "Children live what they learn" was very real. Lawlessness was what the sweet little girl, me, had inherited from my childhood home and the people from my neighborhood. Shame still harbored. Regretfully, my stumbling block was the horrible secrets that I feared would have destroyed my fragile mother, Sue.

Like some young children, On occasion, I slept with my parents and nestled between them. One night, as Sue slept silently, I accidentally touched Harry's penis. The unthinkable happened. I stated, "What is that?" pointing to the penis. I was not redirected and corrected by Harry. He allowed me to touch him and he touched me in the vaginal area. Neither Harry nor Sue ever educated me on boundaries of appropriate touching. From that moment, my childhood was stolen by someone I trusted. Harry began to call me, his five-year-old daughter to the bedroom to touch my private area. Harry would have me sit on him while he was wearing only boxer shorts. Then Harry would have me move around to get dry gratification, while he touched my genitals. As time moved on, Harry began to insert his finger inside of my vagina. Eventually, Harry decided he wanted to have sex with me. Harry used his finger to try to get my vagina to open wider so he could insert his penis, but it would not fit. For some unknown reason, I became fearful, which caused a light bulb to come on in my head.

Due to fear and distrust, I did not want to be left alone with Harry. I feared, hated, and loved Harry, in spite of what he had done to me. I was confused. Between the ages of four and five, I learned how to wear a façade and keep secrets; pretending nothing had happened between Harry and me. It was never discussed. Sue never questioned why I had a change in attitude towards Harry. I often wondered if Sue knew what Harry had been doing to me, while she worked outside of the home. Perhaps, she hoped it would be forgotten and go away. As I progressed in life, the facade, secrecy, and shame were all included in my mental Pandora's Box of confused emotions. I "dressed in normalcy," when I was around Harry, Sue, family, and friends. What commonly seemed wrong to others, appeared to be right and what seemed right to others, was wrong. I was like a zombie, controlled by some unknown evil.

My mental Pandora's Box of secrets was strongly attached and became transparent randomly. I was always trying to change my life's story from sad to "happily ever after."

My new goal was to finish college. By the time I was 21, the shame of being sexually abused as a young child, more than one abortion by random boyfriends, and adultery with two married men had become part of my mental Pandora's Box. As far as the abortions, one of the boyfriends raped me the day I severed the relationship, and a lack of knowledge could be held as my excuse. Yes, I took birth control pills but was always adjusting the pill to accommodate medical issues that were related to taking the pill. There were no patch, day after pill, or some of the other convenient contraceptives. Abstinence should have been practiced, but I was not knowledgeable.

My first teacher, my mother only echoed, "Don't *brang* no baby in this house." The only other examples I had were inside my neighborhood house on "Confusion Lane," the lawless people of the neighborhood and their children that attended the same schools as me. Parenthood was not my choice, but I was willing. However, each potential father refused the idea of fatherhood and paid for the procedure, and I did not believe in forcing the responsibility. No, I did not continue the relationships. The boyfriend that raped me was an addict, and he was trying to force a relationship that I had ended. I witnessed him doing heavy drugs, so it was no hearsay. Relationship annihilation was my way to freedom from his problem. Regrettably, no one told me at less than 12 weeks, there was a living human being inside of me. When it came to marriage, no one educated me that marriage was considered sacred. No one showed or told me how to respect life or marriage. I was a walking testimony of ignorance and perishing on the inside because of a lack of knowledge.

My people are destroyed from lack of knowledge. (Hosea 4:6)

Maybe someone was praying for me because at the age of 23, I decided to change my life. Sometimes, lifestyles could be more visible than we realize. In other words, you never know who may be watching. Could it be possible, God allows us to mess up, just to let us know, choosing right would be impossible, without Him?

There is a way that appears to be right, but in the end it leads to death. (Proverbs 14:12)

After dropping out of college for financial reasons, I worked a couple of odd jobs to save money. One day, I was very discouraged, and I happened to see an ad that Daily Postal Service was hiring. I started imagining how the money could be used and filled out the application. A prayer request was sent to God for help with that endeavor. Although unsaved, I said to God, "I need you to help me to do well on the test to get this job." It happened, I took the test and made a perfect score of 100%. It was hard to believe, but I knew it was God who helped me to be successful.

As it commonly happened after God helped me, I thought about Him, but He was not the center of my life. On a positive side, I had accumulated some convictions. Living by the new beliefs, I saved my money with the intention of returning to college. However, my plans and choices did not line up to what God was allowing to happen in my life. According to Scripture, no one should set goals, without consulting God. In other words, we should always leave room for God to make changes.

Instead, you ought to say, 'If it is the Lord's will, we will live and do this or that.'
(James 4:15)

I got the job at the Daily Postal Service. I lived with my parents for about two years. I was able to pay for furniture and buy a new two-seater sports car. The plans to finish college and purchase a house were not forgotten. Things were going well, but there was no awareness of the old saying, "When God blesses you, the devil will try to steal your blessings," so I was not on guard.

Marriage came, unexpectedly, while pursuing my dreams of finishing college and home ownership. It was beautiful in the beginning. We entered marriage being financially stable, which allowed us to be able to have things we desired. Like other couples, the kids came, which created additional glue to help keep us together when love was not enough. In a matter of time, what seemed secure began to lose its strength due to outside forces. If given power, people, and situations have enough power to steal, kill, and destroy what God had joined in holy matrimony.

My mental Pandora's Box of secrets forcibly accommodated me and an unstable marriage as I accumulated new future experiences. Through the battles of the unknown future, there was someone greater than man, helping me, referred to as the Trinity: God, Jesus, and the Holy Spirit: the all in one team. Many hurdles could have interfered with me finishing college because the demons of my childhood now had new demons that were chasing me. However, there was this soft, gentle voice deep within me saying, "Go back to college." It did not matter what I was doing. The voice would not go away until I enrolled in college to acquire my Bachelor of Science Degree. My response was, "If you want me to return to college then you have to help me choose a college, and if I make less than a 'B' on my assignments, college is not for me." I took action and selected a college.

Everything fell into place, and I did not make less than a "B" except on my last assignment, before graduation. I graduated with a "B" average. While pursuing the goal, my husband and I were separated, and people close to me became sick and died, including Harry. Since Harry defeated death by experiencing near-death accidents that left him with only minor injuries, he chose to return to same behaviors. After becoming a seasoned man, Harry suffered a debilitating illness. His story ended with him battling many sicknesses, going from the hospital to the nursing home. Non-discriminating death that waits dormant to take the young, old, sick, healthy, rich, or poor came to take him when he took his last breath. Before death, Harry never apologized for violating my innocence. I feel he hoped time would erase those memories he could not force himself to resurrect.

Sue stayed a woman of integrity. She was a "ride or die" kind of woman when it came to her husband. Although Sue was free to love again, she refused. She chose to be devoted to Harry, even in his death and faithfully continued to attend church.

As time forced Sue to change, she learned to drive

and found new interests in place of her beloved soap operas, "Lifetime Movies." Sue became a member of a gym, where she participated in activities and became sociable with people in her community, outside of the church. Sue initiated the phrase "I love you," to me and others, but continued to be blunt.

As I continued in pursuit of my goal, despite what was going on around me, it was not easy, but I knew every experience was part of my journey. Every experience was used to help me to have compassion for others. Without a doubt, God's invisible hand had to be present, helping me to be steadfast. With every assignment from God, that still voice, deep within would come to me and inspire me to move towards an assignment that did not seem achievable. I kept reminding myself that I *can* do all things through Christ who strengthens me.

> *When you pass through the waters, I will be with you; and when you pass through the rivers, they will not sweep over you.*
> *When you walk through the fire, you will not be burned; the flames will not set you ablaze.*
> *(Isaiah 43:2)*

Reflection:
Date:
Time:

Reflection:
Date:
Time:

DIVORCE

Divorce came in like a tornado.

I was looking for happiness and was hungry for it. No one should go shopping, while hungry. Looking for the right mate could be treacherous. Some people can be great actors and know how to hide their issues from their childhood and adulthood that caused wounds of brokenness. Emotional wounds can cause a person not to provide trust, loyalty, nor integrity to anyone freely, but desired the character traits for themselves. Most women and men would agree, we are relational beings in search of that perfect mate, our soul-mate, regardless of unresolved issues that may be attached to him or her.

Proper bait must be used to trap someone or something. Just as God can work through someone to fulfill His purpose, Satan can also do the same to try to sabotage the blessings of God. Unfortunately, I had fallen for the glitter of my carnal desires, which opened the door to the evil.

I realize everyone may not agree. Men or women can be good at selling "garnished bullshit sandwiches," excuse my profanity. In other words, some people can be great at selling anything.

I relied on my intuition for everything. Unknowingly, I was behaving self-righteously. I prayed for a husband, but I had not asked God to help me to solve the problem of being able to recognize the man from Him. At that time, I was not aware that God was not the only one able to hear my prayer request. Prayers can be heard by spirits that are not connected to God. Could it be possible, the person I accepted as my mate was an imposter from Satan and not my authentic soul-mate?

No one can judge a book, from the outside looking in. The same analogy can be used for people. He nor I could see the problems attached to us. It was not visible that I had a mental Pandora's Box of issues, nor was he wearing a t-shirt, advertising all the mess attached to him. All we saw was physical appearance, another trap that can be used by Satan to get you derailed into a mess.

While shopping at the car dealership among many people, the man that caused my eyes to wander when I saw him looked to be a charming man, gifted with looks, and had a smile that helped him in his selling. This man had the façade of being a man of integrity. Not doubting he was a man of integrity, but worldly influences can corrupt a person's character. In other words, whatever was being accepted by the world, would be okay. Getting back to what attracted me to him, he had great people skills, and I frequently shopped at the car dealership store for different products. For some supernatural reason, we would always have an encounter. I talked to him about product issues. Coincidentally, I had purchased kitchen appliances, and the products began to shake. He volunteered to bring the missing parts to my apartment. I got to talking to him and realized we both shared the same zodiac sign. A couple of weeks passed; I began to think about him. It was not his looks that were causing the interest; it was his charisma.

The man that caused my eyes to single him out among many shoppers was available and had never been married. I was excited. He could not believe I saw him, among hundreds of people in a car dealership. In my mind, we were a perfect fit, my soul-mate. We exchanged phone numbers. About a week later, we went out on a date. On the first date, I did most of the talking. It was essential to know as much as possible about this seemingly charming man. Weeks passed, and eventually, he phoned and requested another date and many more.

I made a random stop at the used car dealership that sold everything. It was set up like a smorgasbord buffet style restaurant. All the glam made it difficult to determine what was good or bad, so my gambling skills had to be good; otherwise, I was bound to choose something that was not authentic. While browsing, I was reminiscing about my many dates with the man who had caught my eyes. I was sure he was the man that I saw in my prayer. However, my dream had only shown me a silhouette. Maybe I was anxious. He had some personal issues and lacked the full description of the man in my dream. However, I was willing to look beyond the problems and accept him.

When I met him, he was going through some issues that involved the possibility of deception, which could have been viewed as a "Goliath." We married anyway, in spite of some emotional healing that was needed. My advice to him was be prepared for dishonesty because it hurts less. If it turns out this person was honest, continue doing what you were doing. Some truths could break a man's spirit, causing weakness to shine, regardless of how strong he physically appeared to be. Being bamboozled by yesterday's love interest could cause the innocent to become the target of retaliation. It was happening, hurt people hurt people. Did I support him in his "Goliath" moment? Yes. Was it enough? No. He became quiet. Quietness could mean a storm was on its way that included hell.

Soon after being married, I became pregnant with our first daughter and three years later came our second. For a season, I experienced being in love. "For better or worse, 'til death do us part," was my motto.

While he and I continued to be married, secret influences were invading the marriage. Who we were began to show up slowly over the years. Our characters were covered by, "Children live what they learn." We could have made choices that differed from those that influenced us the most, but how could that have been possible, when our models had bragged about grandparents and relatives practicing infidelity. Those people that raised us turned infidelity and divorce into accolades. Our parents, family, relatives, and some of the people we were exposed to were full of chaos that was hidden until they were ready to take off their mask. They were like the lawless people from my childhood neighborhood, and I wondered if I was living my *karma*. Unfortunately, we had confidence in own intuition, which led to more failure, adversities, and demons.

What do you do when the extra drama begins to knock on your door? I do believe we had good intentions, but the lawless people's behaviors of yesterday's past were on our trail. We tried to escape, but we lacked the skills. One of us mirrored the lawlessness of people who lacked skills in problem-solving. The other represented a lack of problem-solving and no shame in divorce or infidelity, which could cremate any glue-bonded marriage. Our intentions were based on good faith. However, we were always defensive, determined not to be hurt by the blows coming at the heart. If only we had known to love God first with all our heart, soul, and mind; just maybe, we would not have been acting like zombies controlled by some unknown evil.

I hated divorce because new relationships require cultivation that was usually not seen until later, regardless of who you chose to share your life with. Warning! The problems included, could be way bigger than the problems you ran from. What happened to the better or worse?

In spite of issues, my goal was to remain married. I was determined to defeat the "Goliath" that I was facing, named, *divorce*. Unfortunately, I lacked listening and communication skills. I was living what I had learned as a child. Having more than enough to meet the needs of the household, was very important, but not enough to sustain the lack harboring behind the scenes of disappointment in the minds of two people. However, if not careful, some drama could destroy anything not rooted and grounded.

Regardless of experience in "relationshipology," marital drama can find the perfect couple. Some drama may be linked to the past or future. I do not know why, but when things seem to be going well, the whiplash of the past or future storm can find you and act like a tornado to demolish the sacred union, created by God. Sometimes love, depending on whether it was conditional or unconditional, can serve as the glue that keeps the marriage from falling apart, while being careful not to be treated like a doormat. Sometimes you have to fight for your marriage, just as you would fight for your life, even if your efforts turn to divorce.

For me, I tried to avoid being prideful and reached out for solutions, such as a pastor, relationship therapy, but divorce was inevitable. It was part of my journey. It was a deep valley that I had to go through. The beauty of the darkness was that I was never alone. My prayer life changed, which provided me with a stronger connection with God, who opened doors to people that were my support. Did I love the man who had given up on us? Yes. But, I had to let him go, so that he could find his happiness. Holding on would have caused deterioration of what was left. Letting go relinquished the invalidation that was festering.

When a simple request would turn into escalation, I would abandon the conversation because criticism would soon follow. Taking a timeout to gather our thoughts would have decreased the tension that was brewing. When the right validation was left out for one another that opened the door for someone else to provide the perfect "love language." Fear caused every word to sound negative. Pride aggressively took over, which left an opening for evil. According to Biblical Scripture, a "house divided will not stand."

Seasonal changes can occur, regardless of anyone's plans. Life can also be viewed the same way. My season changed with many unexpected twists. I did not expect to meet a man who had a steady gaze when he was with me but would wander if he saw a woman when I was not present. Some women would do the same when a man crosses their path. No way would I bash men or women for making a choice that could be causing them to act like some zombie ruled by some unknown evil that was attacking their mind. What was the illusion of the mind that could have been causing a steady negative focus on areas that could have been fixed, such as lack of communication, intimacy, finances, or equality? Some people divorce due to weight gain or extra-marital affairs. Time changes everything, including looks and body images. Can it be possible, better or worse comes with stipulations, no matter how good someone portrays to be? An affair can happen undetected because some people are good at keeping secrets that can affect their image. They know how to plot for years to be together without leaving evidence that could connect them to the scrutiny of an affair.

Divorce came in like a tornado and demolished the years that were filled with ups and downs of life. If I had seen it coming, maybe there would have been some possibilities for survival. Although the climate was perfect for the storm named divorce, it was ignored. I never dreamed it would have done that much damage, leaving behind the debris of bruised emotions and broken hearts. There used to be a time when divorce was frowned upon, just like other closet behaviors. Not to be malicious, was it possible that family and worldly acceptance of divorce had been the environmental influences that orchestrated the path to proceed to undo the "I do"?

Divorce compelled me to go deep in my prayer life because it was so emotionally draining. It was like a dream that had no end. I thought he was the right man. It would have been impossible to know if he was the wrong man, just because our marriage ended in divorce. It was the worldly influences that impacted our marriage, such the related and non-related "friend/enemy" that acted alone or in droves. What I have learned, without God, sooner or later, the calamity of failure will follow. You could blame it on, life happens. Have you ever asked yourself, how can some couples remain married sixty years or more or even until death parted them; could it be a spiritual force greater than man that kept the two souls tied together?

A lot of scenarios could have infested my marriage and opened the door to divorce. Because so many people invited themselves, it became infused with drama. If I could give an exact reason for divorce and provide a guaranteed solution, I would be a millionaire.

Not to expose or offend anyone, what would you do if the following scenarios happened to you that happened to me? Someone phoned your home and voluntarily shared some information that belonged in the trash, but felt privileged to share forbidden secrets that could sabotage any holy matrimony. What would you do? Who would you turn to? Where would you go and how would you handle the situation?

What happens when drama comes with your perfect mate? I had always been told; you cannot hide from your mess. Insecurity and pride can hurt any relationship, but mess will rip it apart. I have learned it would be better to correct major messes before saying, *I do*. All you have to do is ask divorced couples who went through the process that led to an *undo*.

Divorce was never placed on my agenda, regardless of how he had changed. What caused me to avoid the reality that was looking back at me in my mirror, was a denial of the inevitable. I was running from being part of a divorce statistic. Whenever I thought about it, my nights became sleepless, and my peace was stolen. My mind was in a battle with the word divorce. However, I needed a reality check. My paradigm was changing, and I needed a good divorce attorney. The man that caught my eyes among hundreds of people at the car dealership store wanted his freedom so that he could gamble for a chance of newfound happiness.

What caused him to become bedazzled with the idea of freedom of holy matrimony? There were many worldly influences such as family, relatives, friends, strangers, media, even enemies. Some people like to flow with the "in crowd." Some people can be influenced by famous actors, professional athletes, or reality TV. The majority may rule. A man once told me, "A lot of men leave their wives for their girlfriends." The truth may never be known. There could be many other possibilities for me to choose from that helped to "undo the I do," such as some long time awaited lover with a love child or he got tired of going from my bed to her bed, or he got sick of lying.

Something different could be all it takes for some men or women to get blindsided by the grass looking greener on the other side of the fantasy that was the seam ripper that tore right into the relationship being held by a thread. Some men or women would waste no time to tell their spouse it was too late and what was happening was inevitable, while falling for the glitter of infidelity. The fantasy could cause them to lose all respect for marriage by publicly displaying their infidelity. They publically hold their lover's hand, drive their car, travel with them, live with their lover, and even begin another clan of children while being trapped by the piece of paper called a marriage license.

Was my past recycling itself by way of reincarnation? I wondered if my *karma* had come to me dressed in the façade of kindness, love, and integrity, just to siege me in what I was running from, the mental Pandora's Box of secrets and the lawless people.

One truth I know that would not change. Treat others the way you would want someone to treat you. Many have stated, "Payback could be rough."

The evil of yesterday found me, and it was out to get me. It came to my home. I was minding my own business. I had been dodging it for many years. You never know how it will find your location. It would take being strategic and implementing a master plan, just to get past my door. Satan will use anyone as a "Judas," such as a: sister, brother, cousin, child, aunt, uncle, mother, father, teacher, doctor, Christian, mother-in-law, aunt, father-in-law, husband, stepson, brother-in-law, other relatives, and "friend/enemies." They were the perfect strangers perpetrating kindness, love, and integrity. Daily, you can read or hear a sad story on how blood relatives, friends, or strangers inflicted harm against one another or someone innocent.

The lawless people had crossed the threshold of my door. They were all conspiring against my holy matrimony. I was wrestling with the same evil from my childhood home and neighborhood. Everything was being replayed, but with new people and people that I met during my holy matrimony. It was like the scene described in the Bible of Sodom and Gomorrah where any behavior was acceptable, and no one questioned the morality of it all. The strangers would eat my food, watch my TV, and pretend to love the Lord and me. You never know the limitations of people, until boundaries have been crossed that caused confusion, division, and severed relationships. Usually, messes leave behind bruised emotions and broken hearts.

When the perfect strangers who pretended to have my best interest, took off their mask, I was introduced to a new group of lawless people and all of their darkness. Some had been living with their significant other, perpetrating marriage. Many wore shades to cover cloudy eyes that hid their deceitfulness. They consumed copious amounts alcohol regularly and smoked enough cigarettes to cause their teeth to decay. That could have been the reason for their raspy voices.

Once they made up their minds they had to possess something, there was no backing down, for people full of self-pride. The men had mischievous eyes, authoritative voices, and robust white hair. All of them were medium height, stocky, and carrying an alcohol-engorged gut. Even the younger men had white hair and shared the same physical appearances. The men's weakness was transparent by infidelity. Secretly, some of the men were married with young adult children and had been living with their mates for 13 years or more. Sadly, when an authentic spouse died, possibly of bruised emotions and a broken heart, the death would be celebrated by the lovers moving in together. Cohabitation was admired, but to convince someone else's husband or wife to abandon the authentic spouse, was a victory. The two lovers would marry to celebrate. Strangely, after the lovers married the two would become very frail in their health. Still, the people had three or more marriages. That kind of drama could cause anyone to suffer from alcoholism and depression inevitably.

The women were cousins, who were as close as sisters with mirrored personalities. If one of the women did not like you, it also was expressed in the other's behavior towards you. However, some were sneaky; they would pretend to like you, just like typical "friend/enemy." It was all about fitting in to be accepted. The "friend/enemy" wore sunglasses to hide their crossed eyes that took the attention from their full faces. The women were short and very loud. They were known for being great cooks who loved to entertain others with some of their home cooking. Also, they had a gift for entertaining mess too. Their door would always open to extra-marital affairs, including any conceived love child. These women seemed to be kind because they had no problem taking care of their aging mother or father, who lived on a graveled road in the house where families were raised.

Furthermore, the women hid their devious and

malicious ways behind the church, the Bible, and giving. None of their bad behaviors would be present at the initial meeting. Otherwise, anyone in their right mind would have scurried away, even if running backward was needed from the dysfunctional people, who were like the people from the lawless neighborhood of my past, full of drama. I had experienced foolishness in my family, as a child. Therefore, I could have easily removed myself from their foolishness. I did not understand their ways because they were mature people entertaining evil while being over fifty.

The younger women were known for their oval faces, deceptive eyes, and naturally long red hair with a gray streak in the bang area. They were attention getters because of their full-figured and shapely bodies. They had no problem with the drama that included a love child. Their strategy was to maintain long-term affairs with men by convincing them to be a best friend.

Livid would describe the anger that would brew in any authentic wife's mind. That kind of behavior could bruise any lady's emotions and break her heart, as it did mine. These women were ruthless. Their goal was to get rid of an authentic wife, like me. Some of them were brazen enough to phone my home and tell me about the affair, not leaving out the graphic details of the sexual encounter and the love child they shared with my husband. They refused to do a blood test to prove the authenticity of the love child, despite the child being younger than my last child who was only six weeks old when I witnessed my husband's vasectomy. I saw the doctor clip and burn the so-called hero's, vas deferens tubes. If that did not work, the other lawless people would assist in the sabotage by listening in on the conversation by three-way to help in the mission. To assure victory, they would advertise, using any tactics needed to get the attention of those who needed to be eliminated.

The new lawless people were outlaws from hell. No sacrifice was made to avoid bruising emotions and breaking hearts. Maybe the lawless people behaviors were a continuous cycle of "Children live what they learn." You would think, someone mature in age, over fifty would have been trying to redirect others from creating a pit. However, I did hear one of the mature lawless people state, while personal chaos was happening in their life, "This is just life." There was no connection made between behavior and consequences.

How did I feel? I was furious, hurt, and wanted each invader to experience the same drama that crossed the threshold of my door. Some people could cause you to want to incarcerate them, to avoid their corruption.

What I have learned, it does not matter how far you run from your past; it can find you. That could be by way of affairs, adultery, incest, abuse, fake people, etc. My mental Pandora's Box could not be buried deep enough for me to escape. The people I feared losing, betrayed and judged me for the sake of anything goes.

My regret was not praying to God on how to handle every situation. He would have given me wisdom and peace, as he orchestrated the outcome. I wondered if the whiplash of my past had come after me because I never told anyone the secrets inside of my mental Pandora's Box. By the grace and mercy of God, hearts began to heal. Human grace and mercy were not easy but given to those who were downright ugly. Just like me, eventually, their *karma* will seek them out too, using the perfect bait.

Before the evil that found me, I could recall a time when he would tell me, *I love you* and would give me flowers without reason. No one had ever said, "I love you," except him and our girls. When the girls began to talk, they would say "I love you," on a regular basis. It was like God was trying to fill that void I had missed out on, as a child. It might sound foolish, but I asked why he gave me flowers. Then, I went on to ask my little girls and him, "Why do you say, I love you?" I was living what I had learned; no one said, *"I love you"* when I was a child. I experienced a great season of love because no special occasion was missed. He always remembered birthdays, valentine's day, anniversaries, Mother's Day, and Christmas. Whenever events came to the city, such as comedy shows, concerts, and going dancing, he made a point to entertain me. Also, he loved entertaining guests in the home. We would prepare a full course meal, play music, cards, laugh and talk. It was not just about us; we would include our daughters on movie night. Everyone would choose a movie from, "Time Out Movie Depot." Later, we all watched each other's movies. He seemed grounded because there were no problems visible; occasionally going to church with the family, going to work and returning home, and paying the bills. He kept up his routine. I would tell him jokingly; he missed his calling of being an actor. Out of the blue, he created an argument over my comment of desiring us to spend more time together. That was his excuse to leave me. "Yes," it was more to his actions. He had a secret, "honey hole," pulling his chains. He and his latest secret were conspiring ways to be together. They shared with my oldest daughter at a Christmas gathering they had a love child, who attended the same community college as my daughter. I was not at all surprised.

    Despite what I was feeling, I got thrust out of my routine of allowing him to disrespect me and demonstrating the wrong examples to our daughters, just because he could not say, "no," to affairs that included unprotected sex and the debris of love children.

God was allowing my life plans to change for my good.

There was nothing I could have humanly done that would have changed my situation. I had to continue to move forward in the many experiences that were ahead of me. It was trusting in God's timing in my life and letting go of those things that were once familiar. Did the husband ever try to return to the relationship? He came back three times, offering me a role in his latest drama. I could not believe what was offered, considering the drama I had experienced, during the marriage. I was offended initially, did a quick prayer, adjusted my thinking and attitude and realized he was still walking around like a zombie being ruled by some unknown evil.

Fortunately for me, I knew God had not sent him back because nothing being offered in reconciliation, included being done properly and orderly. His best offer was secrecy, confusion, and drama. My yesterday that included him was gone, and I decided to let him and his drama go. I refused to go back to a man who had not repented of his old ways of collecting messes. Do I believe in second chances? Yes, but not chaos. Therefore, I rejected the offer. Like that old saying, "bad decisions make great memories." Some people are narcissistic, and some men are ruled by their little head that has no brain.

Bettina J.D. Woodard

Reflection:
Date:
Time:

BARS

Reflection:
Date:
Time:

_____

_____

_____

_____

_____

_____

_____

_____

_____

_____

_____

_____

_____

_____

FREEDOM

*My experiences were horrific,
but I survived!*

Is love just a pipe dream that most humans spend a great deal of their life searching for, just to discover the partnership was based on a fantasy built on stipulations? In other words, if you fail to fulfill my fantasy, you will no longer receive my integrity, honor, compassion, respect, and patience. Why is it so impossible to love a stranger you just met with the same integrity you would want someone to love you or someone dear to your heart.

Relationship rules are similar to purchasing an item under contract. If it fails to operate or loses its appeal, it will be replaced or discarded, regardless of the years of service, a reason for everyone to guard his or her heart.

Is it possible to genuinely love yourself and not hate your enemy, without loving God first? Based on the following Scriptures, nothing should come before God, not your parents, children, friends, relatives, spouse, boyfriend, girlfriend, or significant other. Even more important, be careful how you treat others because sooner or later the good or bad will boomerang back to you.

> *Love the Lord your God with all your heart, and with all your soul, and with all your mind. This is the first and greatest commandment. And the second is like it: love your neighbor as yourself. (Matthew 22:37-39)*

So in everything, do to others what you would have them do to you, for this sums up the Law and the Prophets. (Matthew 7:12)

When a shift occurred within what was left of my family, it was excruciating. While I was walking in the shadow of the unknown and simultaneously encouraging my daughters who were looking at me, their new hero, it was hard to overlook fear, that accompanied the new changes. To annihilate fear, I reminded myself; God is, was, and will be part of every change. As a result of my paradigm shift, I was released from people and situations that were not going to be part of my new season. I walked in forgiveness, forgiving myself first, and then others. It took time for me to be able to look back, without bitterness toward people that played a role in my bruised emotions, broken heart, and additional shame. As I walked in my destiny, set up by the intentional God, I experienced happiness and disappointments.

Things were looking upward; I was getting resettled after the divorce. I made plans to resurrect an old home into a livable rooftop so my daughters and I could have a place to live. I was introduced to a contractor who portrayed himself to be an upstanding Christian. He had a façade as a pillar of the community. He often commented on his regular attendance at church, Sunday school, and claimed to be a cheerful giver.

This man was a smooth talker, displaying kindness, which seemed authentic. To back up his selling, he drove me to homes and a church that was finished or close to being completed. He would unlock the door of each building and give a tour. I now question whether he showed me his work or someone else's.

After I had given him money to begin the work according to the contract, everything changed. Regular inspections to meet the building code laws did not take place as was agreed. Also, when questioned, he reminded me he had been a contractor for three decades. He shifted from being married to propositioning sexual favors. I had to remind him of his position and my respect for his wife who was not present. The rejection was not received very well. The quality of his work shifted to worthless. He was constructing a non-livable shell, while I continued to pay a mortgage, storage bill, and other related expenses. This man was a wolf in sheep's clothing.

I was tricked by his façade of being a Christian. Deception bamboozled me because I had a dream and desired to see it happen quickly. Apparently, I was moving ahead of God, which included failures and losses. Yes, I prayed about what I wanted, but there were others who also influenced my decision, adding more pressures to move hastily. And probably they were not prayerful about the advice they gave me or did not have a relationship with God, to lead and direct them with wisdom and discernment.

The financial setback caused my daughters and me to live out of our vehicles, storage unit, and my mother's two-bedroom one-bathroom home. It has been a living nightmare.

While my daughters and I have been going through the shadow of the unknown, pressing forward has remained our mindset. God's promises revealed to me; I had to forgive those who hurt me, to receive forgiveness. Immediately, I remembered my past mistakes and used my free will to walk in forgiveness. What seemed to be a failure, was a real victory. Although everything was not as I desired, our needs were met. We had a place to stay, food, health, friends, family, transportation, employment, and attorney fees for the new battle. Some attorneys will even fight *pro bono*.

Sometimes, blessing can come in the size of a tiny mustard seed, which is hard to see. This is the same requirement God expects of our faith.

> *...if you have faith as small as a mustard seed, you can say to this mountain, 'Move from here to there,' and it will move. Nothing will be impossible for you. (Matthew 17:20)*

In all the chaos of my life, God, Jesus, and the Holy

Spirit were with me. Because of their presence, I was strengthened, healed, restored, and delivered. As I recalled my devious ways as a young adult, my ways were similar to those who brought shame, dishonor, division, and confusion to my household. Sometimes people tend to forget their dirty deeds. However, when, "the tables turn," it can give you a "flashback whiplash."

Whenever one of the individuals that played a role in my many adversities came to my mind, I lifted that person up in prayer and meditated continuously on God's promises.

After my various life experiences and becoming a parent, my free will was used to educate my children on boundaries, listening, communication, and problem-solving. I chose not to be like the people of the lawless neighborhood or the new people who brought hurt and shame into my life. I had an understanding of being lost in sin, which can cause you to walk around like a zombie, controlled by some unknown evil.

My greatest epiphany: When I gave everything to the God of second chances, all the baggage in the mental Pandora's Box in exchange for His peace, "The peace of God, which transcends all understanding, will guard your hearts and your minds in Christ Jesus." (Philippians 4:7)

Free will is our gift from God, so it is up to you, how you use it. Be bold, confident, and have courage.

Do not hide your stories that have held you, hostage, due to self-sabotage or the sabotage of others. Likewise, be willing to share stories of God's goodness. As long as life exists in our bodies, we will be part of a story. Someone might be waiting for you to plant a mustard seed story that will help to set them free from the incarceration of their mind.

I could have allowed what appeared to be failed circumstances to control my attitude. Instead, I pressed on facing each "Goliath" with the invisible hand of God. Thankfully, the God of order and not confusion used His creativity to remove some people, and blocked some situations, to carry out the plans and purposes for my life. If I had not given all of my baggage in the mental Pandora's Box to God, in exchange for His peace, I would have given my victory to my foes and not had this story to share, to help others. The all-knowing God brought me to humility, while He held me with His righteous right hand. He lifted me up when I fell and rescued me from wandering in the wilderness.

And we know that all things God works for the good for those who love him, who have been called according to His purpose. (Roman 8:28)

According to John 10:10 "The thief comes to steal, kill and destroy. God comes that they may have life, and have it to the full." My experiences were horrific, but I survived. People in the Bible experienced challenges too: Abraham, Joseph, and Job. Their stories are recorded to inspire and teach us to trust God. Abraham obeyed God and left his native land and all he knew to travel to an unknown land. Joseph was sold into slavery by his brothers and left for dead. Job suffered the loss of his children, servants, and wealth. God restored each man to a better position after their trials.

> *Forget the former things, do not dwell on the past. See, I am doing a new thing! Now it springs up; do you not perceive it? I am making a way in the wilderness and streams in the wasteland. (Isaiah 43: 18, 19)*

Living forward can be difficult if your past is holding you hostage. Lot's wife looked back and turned into a pillar of salt, (Genesis 19:26). If you are willing to let go of the former things, God will give a second chance for anyone including the murderer, prisoner, divorcee, abortionist, abuser, homosexual, and female/male prostitute.

I often wonder, does *karma* find you as a descendant? If this is true, you can make any choice you like. However, the consequences or the penalties may affect someone innocent.

Some people allow jealousy and envy to dictate

their character, which may lead to stealing, killing, and destroying their life and the lives of others. Face it; life will never be perfect. Otherwise (God) the Creator of everything, would not be needed.

Having new a vision allows me to see beyond the exterior of my broken plans. In other words, I am using my free will not to look back, but look forward to what God has for me. Keeping God's promises in my heart is how I abort the lies of Satan. We all have a unique Promise Land. Most people miss what God has for them because they are on the "outside looking in" at what others appear to have. Another epiphany: We all have some lack, which can steal our focus causing us to forfeit our prize. One of the Ten Commandments states: "Thou shalt not covet." (Exodus 20:17)

> *The Lord Almighty has sworn: 'Surely as I have planned, so will it be; and as I have purposed, so shall it stand.' (Isaiah 14:24)*

My inspiration came from knowing the pleasant, unpleasant, and downright ugly would not last forever. The Almighty God was always in control. Even though at times, life experiences felt like extreme cruelty, each experience was temporary.

The Serenity Prayer is a powerful tool that helped me walk peacefully through life.

> *God, grant me the Serenity to accept the things I cannot change, the courage to change the things I can, the wisdom to know the difference.*

"Success," said Winston Churchill, "is going from failure to failure without loss of enthusiasm."

This is the day the Lord has made. I shall rise from my bed, rejoice, and be glad in it. Unfortunately, no one can go back in time and change their past, but anyone can choose to let yesterday's mistakes be a guide for tomorrow's better choices. Whether you believe in Jehovah God or not, He is, was, and will be in charge of each season of my life and yours. Yay, I rise to "Free at Last."

Reflection:
Date:
Time:

Reflection:
Date:
Time:

SCRIPTURES ON FORGIVENESS

"If my people, who are called by my name, will humble themselves and pray and seek my face and turn from their wicked ways, then I will hear from heaven, and I will forgive their sins and will heal their land." (2 Chronicles 7:14)

"You Lord, are forgiving and good, abounding in love to all who call to you." (Psalm 86:5)

"No longer will they teach their neighbor, or say to one another, 'know the Lord,' because they will all know me, from the least of them to the greatest, declares the Lord. "For I will forgive their wickedness and will remember their sin no more." (Jeremiah 31:34)

"Then Peter came to Jesus and asked, 'Lord, how many times shall I forgive my brother or sister who sins against me? Up to seven times?' Jesus answered, 'I tell you, not seven times, but seventy-seven times.' (Matthew 18: 21, 22)

"Have faith in God," Jesus answered, 'Truly I tell you, if anyone says to this mountain, 'Go, throw yourself into the sea,' and does not doubt in their heart but believes that what they say will happen, it will be done for them. Therefore, I tell you, whatever you ask for in prayer, believe that you received it, and it will be yours and when you stand praying, if you hold anything against anyone, forgive them, so that your Father in heaven may forgive you your sins." (Mark 11:22- 25)

"The Pharisees and the teachers of the law began thinking to themselves, who is this fellow who speaks blasphemy? Who can forgive sins but God alone?" (Luke 5:21)

"You, Lord, showed favor to your land; you restored the fortunes of Jacob. You forgave the iniquity of your people and covered all their sins. You set aside all your wrath and turned from your fierce anger." (Psalm 85:1, 2, 3)

"Whoever is not with me is against me, and whoever does not gather with me scatters. And so, I tell you, every kind of sin can be forgiven, but blasphemy against the Spirit will not be forgiven. Anyone who speaks a word against the Son will be forgiven, but anyone who speaks against the Holy Spirit will not be forgiven, either in this age or in the age to come." (Matthew 12:30, 31, 32)

"Which is easier: to say, 'Your sins are forgiven,' or to say, 'Get up and walk?' But I want you to know that the Son of Man has the authority on earth to forgive sins." (Luke 5:23)

"Get rid of all bitterness, rage, and anger, brawling and slander, along with every form of malice. Be kind and compassionate to one another, forgiving each other, just as in Christ God forgave you." (Ephesians 4:31, 32)

"Humble yourselves before the Lord, and he will lift you up." (James 4:10)

Reflection:
Date:
Time:

BARS

Reflection:
Date:
Time:

HEALING SCRIPTURES

"And the God of all grace, who called you to his glory in Christ, after you have suffered a little while, will himself restore you and make you strong, firm and steadfast." (1Peter 5:10)

"My grace is sufficient for you, for my power is made perfect in weakness." (2 Corinthians 12:9)

"The Lord is my shepherd, I lack nothing. He makes me lie down in green pastures, He leads me beside quiet waters, he refreshes my soul. He guides me along the right paths for his name's sake. Even though I walk through the darkest valley, I will fear no evil, for you are with me; your rod and your staff, they comfort me. You prepare a table before me in the presence of my enemies. You anoint my head with oil; my cup overflows. Surely your goodness and love will follow me all the days of my life, and I will dwell in the house of the Lord forever." (Psalm 23)

"The righteous cry out, and the Lord hears them; he

delivers them from all their troubles. The Lord is close to the brokenhearted and saves those who are crushed in spirit." (Psalm 34:17, 18)

"And we know that in all things God works for the good of those who love him, who have been called according to his purpose." (Romans 8:28)

"Do you not know that your bodies are temples of the Holy Spirit, who is in you, whom you have received from God? You are not your own; you were bought at a price. Therefore, honor God with your bodies."
(1 Corinthians 6:19, 20)

"For the Spirit God gave us does not make us timid, but gives us power, love, and self-discipline."
(2Timothy 1:7)

"May you be blessed by the Lord, the Maker of heaven and earth." (Psalm 115:15)

"So we say with confidence, The Lord is my helper; I will not be afraid. What can mere mortals do to me?" (Hebrews 13:6)

"My son, pay attention to what I say; turn your ear to my words. Do not let them out of your sight, keep them within your heart; for they are life to those who find them and health to one's whole body." (Proverbs 20:20-22)

"He is my loving God and my fortress, my stronghold and my deliverer, my shield, in whom I take refuge, who subdues peoples under me." (Psalm 144:2)

"He heals the brokenhearted and binds up their wounds." (Psalm 147: 3)

Reflection:
Date:
Time:

_____

_____

_____

_____

_____

_____

_____

_____

_____

_____

_____

_____

_____

_____

BARS

Reflection:
Date:
Time:

NATIONAL STATISTICS ON CHILD ABUSE

"In 2015, approximately 1,670 children died from abuse and neglect in the United States. In 2015, Children's Advocacy Centers around the country served more than 311,000 child victims and their families. The Ages served: 0-6 37%, 7-12 37%, 13-17 26%. Nearly, 700,000 children are abused in the U.S. annually. 3.4 million children received an investigation or alternative response from child protective service. 2.3 million Children received prevention services."

"Young children were more susceptible to maltreatment. Neglect is the most common form of maltreatment. Children in the first year of their life had the highest rate of victimization of 24.2 per 1,000 children in the national population of the same age. Four out of five abusers are the victims of parents. The parent was the perpetrator of 78.1%, child maltreatment cases. Two-thirds of children served disclosed sexual abuse (205,438). Nearly 20% of children served, disclosed physical abuse (60,897). 211,831 children received on-site forensic interviewing at a Children's Advocacy Center. People investigated

were children between the ages of 13 to 17, parent or caregiver, and those related to the child victim."
http://www.nationalchildrenalliance.org/media

The Effects of Childhood Abuse on Adults

"Both men and women may experience a wide variety of symptoms that may be associated with a history of childhood sexual abuse. The cause of these symptoms is not recognized by the physician or patient."

"For the survivors of childhood sexual abuse, there is minimal compromises to their adult functioning. Others will have myriad psychological, physical, and behavioral symptoms because of their abuse."

"Adult survivors have disproportionately high use of health care services, more severe symptoms with more complex patterns of presentation, and often somatic symptoms which represent psychological distress that manifests itself as bodily ailments that do not respond to routine treatment. These issues can create frustration for women and men and treatment challenges for their physicians."

The Meaning of Childhood Abuse

"Childhood sexual abuse can be defined as any exposure to sexual acts imposed on children who inherently lack the emotional, maturational, and cognitive development to understand or to consent to such acts. These acts do not always involve sexual intercourse or physical force; rather, they involve manipulation and trickery. Authority and power enable the perpetrator to coerce the child into compliance. Characteristics and motivations of perpetrators of childhood sexual abuse vary: some may act out sexually to exert dominance over another individual; others may initiate the abuse for their own sexual gratification."

"Although the definition of child abuse may vary from state to state, most agree that abusive sexual contact can include breast and genital fondling, oral and anal sex, and vaginal intercourse. Even non-contact coercion to watch sexual acts or posing in child pornography has become part of the definition of child abuse."

"The exact number of childhood abuse in the United States is unknown, due to the shame and disgrace affiliated with abuse. Most victims never share their experience. Research has found that victims come from all cultural, racial, and economic groups."

http://www.healthplace.com/about-healthyplace/authors/samatha-fluck-biography

To report suspected cases of child abuse, please call 1-800-422-4453.

BARS

NOTES

ABOUT THE AUTHOR

Bettina lives in the beautiful mountainous area of Tennessee. Her accomplishments include raising two daughters, acquiring a Bachelor of Science Degree in Organizational Management, and becoming an author. She enjoys family, friends, traveling, dancing, a variety of music genres, reading short stories, and being part of a team that helps others.

Although Bettina has been viewed as extraordinary because of her courage, confidence, and boldness to share a compelling true story; she sees herself as being a typical person.

A story was locked inside of Bettina waiting for the right time to break free, to go public to plant a real-life story seed for those who need it. Bettina's new outlook helped her to trample her fear by sharing the pleasant, unpleasant, and downright ugly stories to help someone launch into their freedom from an incarcerated mind trapped by hidden secrets of yesterday.

www.ingramcontent.com/pod-product-compliance
Lightning Source LLC
LaVergne TN
LVHW022323080426
835508LV00041B/2091